Totty

Zeidy

Bubby

Mommy

Yanky

Malky

Meet the
Mitzvah
Kinder®
Family

Yossi

Surele

Moishy

Feter Fishel

Hershy

Baby Esty

Baby Chaim

Tovya

Mendy

Shloimy

Mendy

Tante Blimy

Chesky

Reb Shmuel

Mr. Kapalovsky

Rav

Rebetzin

Mrs. Brull

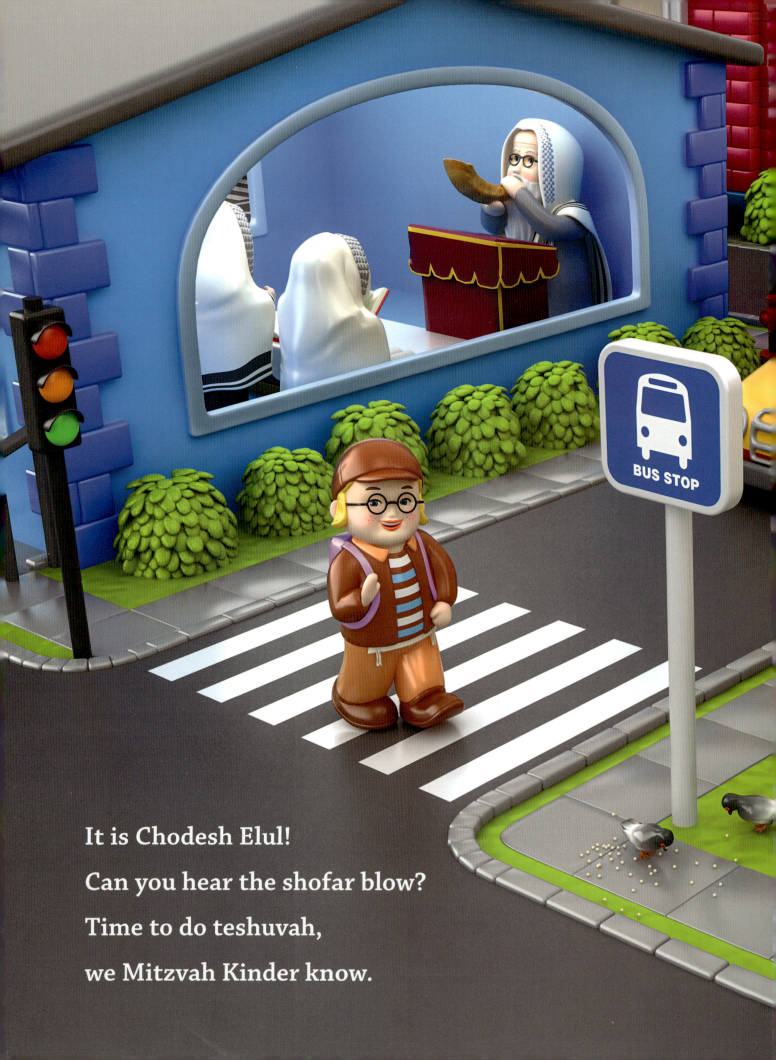

It is Chodesh Elul!

Can you hear the shofar blow?

Time to do teshuvah,

we Mitzvah Kinder know.

Beep! Beep! Beep! The bus is here.

We are all excited to start a new year.

The Rebbe brings a scale for us boys to see,

and explains that Hashem weighs each deed carefully.

The Rebbe asks Yanky, "How can our mitzvahs tip the scale?"

"By doing teshuvah, tefillah and tzedakah without fail!"

Morah gives us children crayons to paste and color.

We create L'shana Tova cards for our father and mother.

Dear Zeidy and Bubby,

I want to wish you a good year, you should be healthy and see lots of nachas from me.

Love,

Malky

The mailman greets Zeidy and gives him a letter.
Bubby puts on her glasses so she can read it better.
"A L'shana Tova card from Malky!" Zeidy is delighted.
"Let's read it together," says Bubby, all excited.

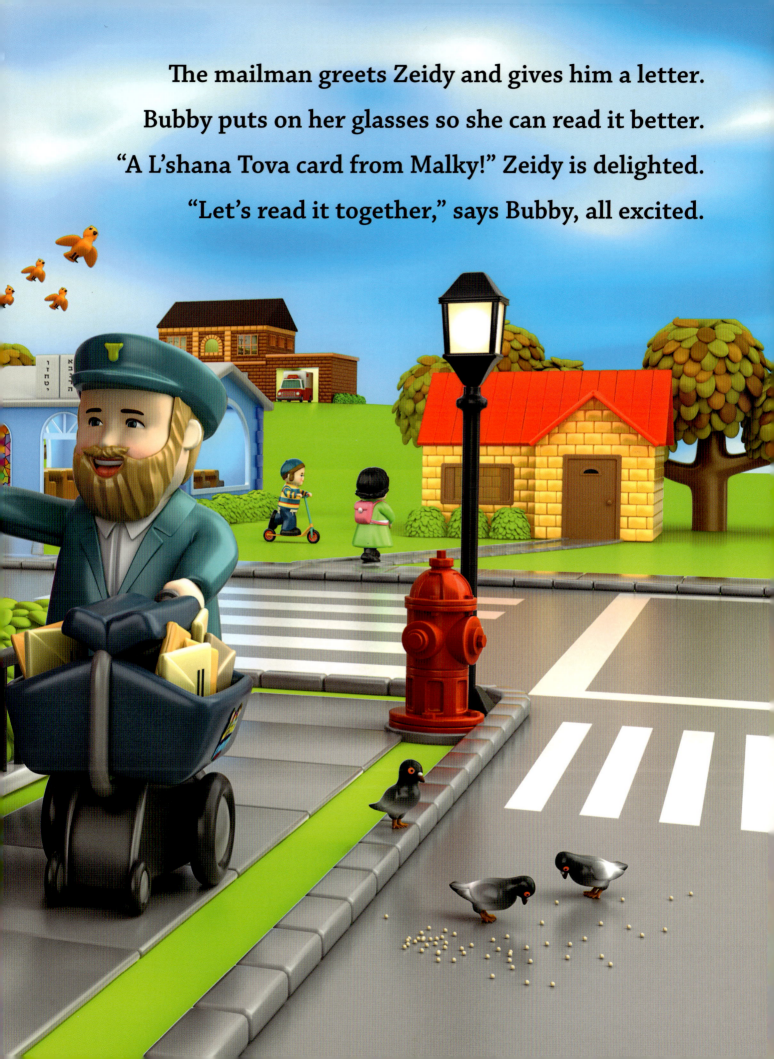

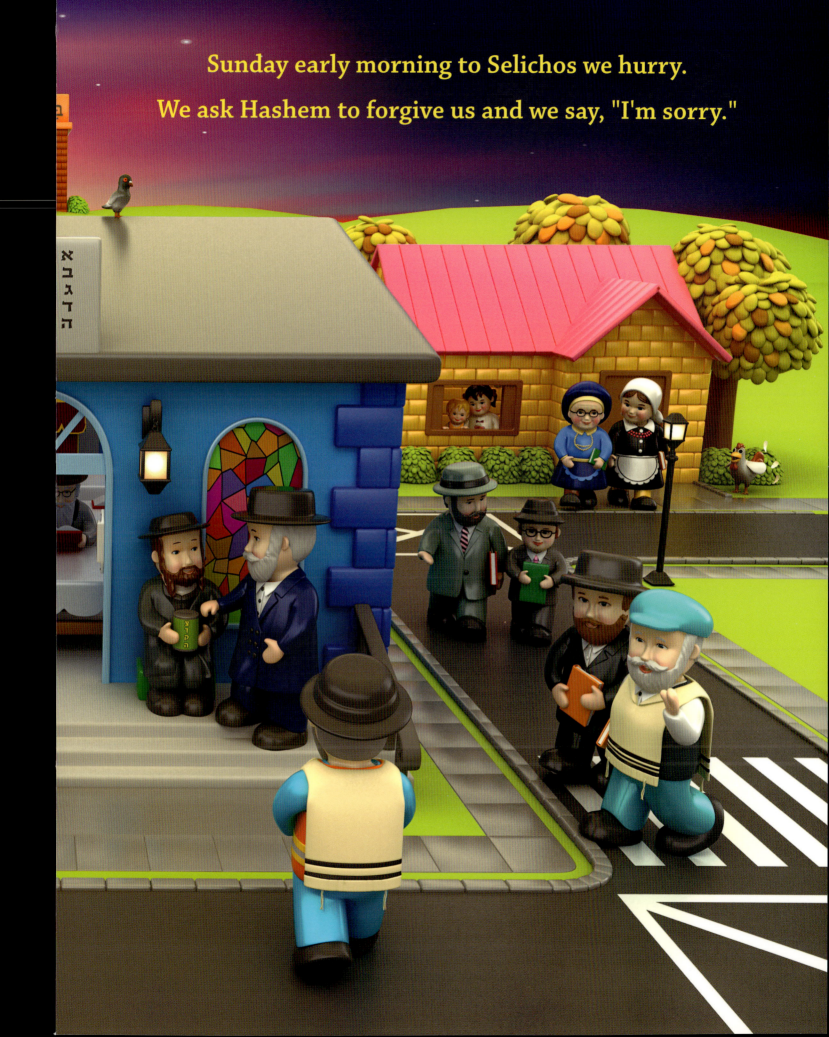

Sunday early morning to Selichos we hurry.

We ask Hashem to forgive us and we say, "I'm sorry."

To the Mitzvah Kinder market we run,
shopping for yom tov is so much fun.

Apples, honey, carrots and more,

we help Mommy bring the bags to the door.

Before Rosh Hashanah,
we help Mommy bake,
yummy round challahs,
honey cookies, and cake.

On Rosh Hashanah we wish each other a bracha,
"L'shana Tova" for our friends and mishpacha.

We dip apple in honey, eat the head of a fish.

Sweet carrots and pomegranate
we taste from the dish.

On Rosh Hashanah we go to shul to hear,
The sound of the shofar, loud and clear.
We say "Amen" to the bracha out loud,
"Tootoo! Let's do teshuva
and make Hashem proud!"

The rebbe takes us boys to the pond nearby.

We say Tashlich and ask Hashem, "Please hear our cry."

We throw away our averois and know for sure,

we are starting the new year, fresh and pure.

Totty swings the kaparah over Malky's head.

"Quack! Quack! Quack!" Malky starts to fret.

"Malky dear, please don't fear.

Our averois go to the kaparah and we'll have a good year."

Erev Yom Kippur we ask each other,

"Please forgive me, sister and brother."

"Chaim, do you know that on Yom Kippur
we wash only our fingers?"
"Yes, Malky," says Chaim, "and I know too,
we don't wear a leather shoe!"

Mommy is fasting and davening all day,
with Baby Esty and Chaim we Mitzvah Kinder play.

Mr. Kapalovsky, Uncle Fishel, Tovya and R' Shmuel,

all dressed like malachim when they come to shul.

Everyone davens with tears in their eyes,

"Hashem, please, listen to our cries."

אָסוּר לְדַבֵּר
בִּשְׁעַת
הַתְּפִילָה

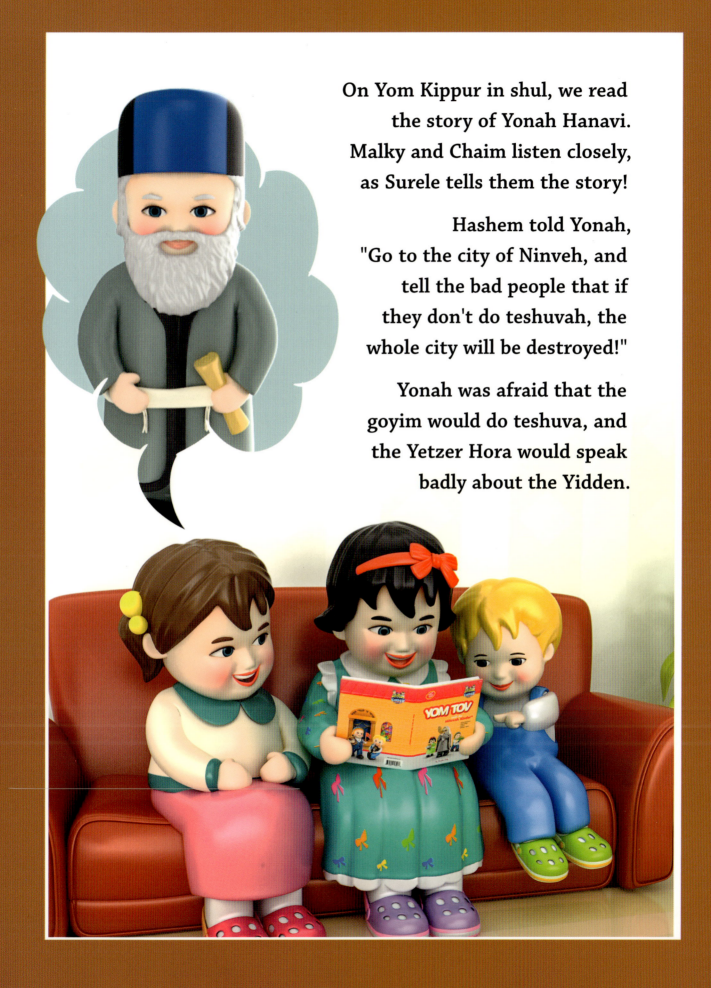

On Yom Kippur in shul, we read the story of Yonah Hanavi. Malky and Chaim listen closely, as Surele tells them the story!

Hashem told Yonah, "Go to the city of Ninveh, and tell the bad people that if they don't do teshuvah, the whole city will be destroyed!"

Yonah was afraid that the goyim would do teshuva, and the Yetzer Hora would speak badly about the Yidden.

5 Look! All the other ships are sailing calmly. The storm is only over our ship! Somebody on this ship probably acted badly!

6 Yonah, wake up! Our ship is sinking! Daven to Hashem! Only He can save us!

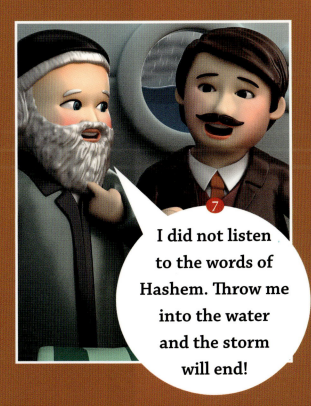

7 I did not listen to the words of Hashem. Throw me into the water and the storm will end!

8 The people on the ship threw Yonah overboard.

Come, Yonah. Hashem has sent me to swallow you. You will be very comfortable inside me. When you look through my eyes, you will see the wondrous plants and fish that Hashem created deep in the sea.

Yonah was so happy to be in the big bright fish that he forgot to daven to Hashem! Hashem made the big fish spit him out. Then a small fish came along and swallowed him.

Ouch! It is so squishy in here! Oh, Hashem! Help me! I want to live and do your precious mitzvos!

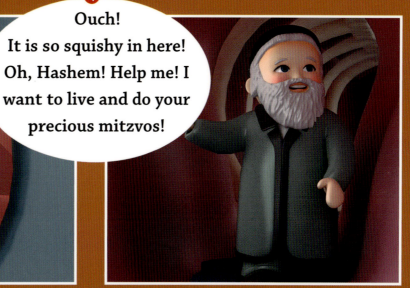

The small fish spit Yonah out onto dry land.

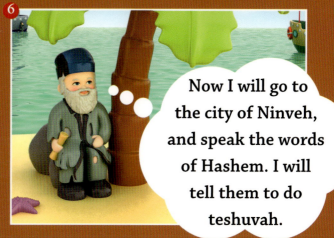

Now I will go to the city of Ninveh, and speak the words of Hashem. I will tell them to do teshuvah.

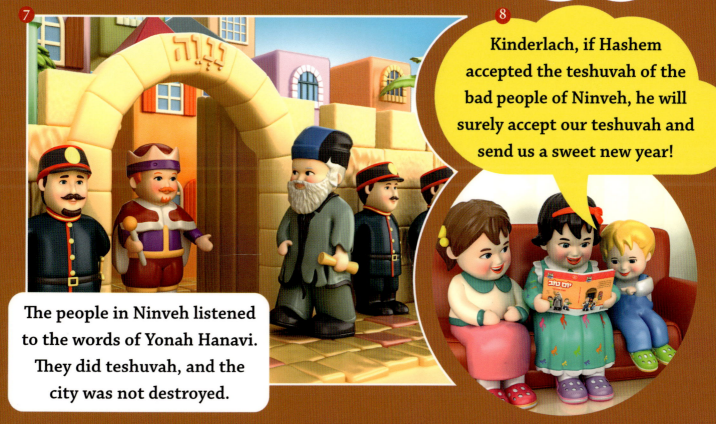

The people in Ninveh listened to the words of Yonah Hanavi. They did teshuvah, and the city was not destroyed.

Kinderlach, if Hashem accepted the teshuvah of the bad people of Ninveh, he will surely accept our teshuvah and send us a sweet new year!

We Mitzvah Kinder prepare for Sukkos happily.
Tovi cuts the twigs off the tree carefully.
Pinchus carries schach, Chesky drills the boards tight,
Malky hangs the decorations, Moishy brings the light.
"Our Sukkah is almost ready," Chaim shouts with glee.
Totty buys a nice esrog that we all want to see.

The yom tov Sukkos is a time of joy,

for all the Mitzvah Kinder, girl and boy.

Up in the air, round and round,

Bump, bump, bump, we touch the ground.

On Chol Hamoed we have fun on the rides,

spending time with our cousins on swings and slides.

Simchas Torah we dance all night in shul,

with Zeidy and Totty, the Rav and Reb Shmuel.

We kiss the Torah and dance in a ring.

"Tov li Toras pichah" together we sing.

Moishy says a brachah on the Torah loud and clear.

We catch the candies flying through the air.

We say "Hamalach hagoal" and ask Hashem for a bracha,

"May we learn Torah all year with lots of hatzlacha."

**Mitzvah Kinder®
Shabbos Book**

**Mitzvah Kinder®
Yom Tov Book - Yiddish**

**Mitzvah Kinder®
Pesach Book**

**Mitzvah Smileys™
Sticker Collection**

**Mitzvah Kinder®
Jigsaw Puzzles**

**Mitzvah Kinder®
Refuah Shleima
Mentchees**

**Shabbos with the
Mitzvah Kinder®**

**Mitzvah Kinder®
Community Mentchees**

**Mitzvah Kinder®
Neighbors**

Mitzvah Kinder® Cousins

Mitzvah Kinder® Family

Find Mitzvah Kinder® at your local toy store | www.MitzvahKinder.com